© Cherry Gilchrist 1983
First published 1983
All rights reserved. No part of this publication
may be reproduced, in any form or by any means,
without permission from the Publisher

Typeset by Tek-Art Ltd, London SE20
and printed in Great Britain by
R. J. Acford
Chichester, Sussex
for the publishers
Batsford Academic and Educational Ltd, an imprint
of B. T. Batsford Ltd,
4 Fitzhardinge Street
London W1H 0AH

ISBN 0 7134 1366 2

ACKNOWLEDGMENT

The Author would like to thank Angharad
North and Steven North for general research
assistance; and the following people for their
help in recalling working conditions of the
past, or for advising on modern methods and
technology: *Shops*: Leah North; *Factories*:
Fred Derrett, Mary Moorcroft, Stan Snell;
Transport: Graham Bell, Paul Fawcett;
Farming: Alf Heywood; *Housework*:
Kathleen Phillips; *Mining*: Cyril Williamson;
Offices: Richard Phillips, David Wootten.

The Author and Publishers would like to
thank the following for their kind permission
to reproduce copyright illustrations:
Barnaby's Picture Library, figs 3, 44, 45, 46,
56, 57, 60; Beamish North of England Open
Air Museum, figs 1, 13, 48, 50, 51, 52;
British Airways, fig 29; BBC Hulton Picture
Library, figs 39, 41, 54; British Railways
Board, fig 25; *Farmers Weekly*, figs 37, 38;
Ford of Britain, figs 21, 22, 55, 58, 59;
House of Fraser, figs 5, 9, 10, 11; National
Coal Board, figs 49, 53; North Western
Museum of Science and Industry, figs 18,
20; Popperfoto, figs 2, 42; Sainsbury's, figs 4,
6, 7, 8, 12, 14, 17, 26, 27, 28; Josiah
Wedgwood and Sons Ltd, figs 15, 16, 23.
The other pictures are from the Publishers'
collection.

Contents

The Illustrations

1
The Changing Patterns of Work

Work is a central issue in our lives. It provides us with the money that we need to live on, takes up about one third of our waking lives, and can make or mar our general health and happiness. In the 1980s, the population of Britain is more conscious of work than for many decades. High unemployment means that work is in short supply; rapidly advancing technology is altering the structure of many jobs beyond recognition. It is helpful to look at the present situation in the context of a longer period of time, to see the pattern behind these changes and to discover how today's ways of work differ from those of fifty years ago.

This book sets out to study seven different kinds of work and to follow them through from the 1930s until the present day. It would be more accurate to describe these seven as "categories" of work rather than as "jobs"; the category of office work, for instance, would include people employed in jobs as typists, accountants, executives and so on. Together, these seven categories represent a broad cross-section of work carried out in Britain over the last half-century, and give us enough examples to see how British working life itself has altered during this time.

Before going on to explore specific occupations, some of the general factors which can influence employment will be discussed.

New Inventions

One of the most obvious ways in which a person's job can be affected is when new machinery or equipment is introduced. Right from the Stone Age man has developed tools with which he may do a job more easily — he discovered that a stone knife is more efficient for cutting up a bison than his bare hands, for instance! Man's ingenuity leads him on to make further experiments and discoveries, and these, ultimately, affect the kind of work that is done and the way it is carried out. When tractors were introduced, for example, replacing horses, the whole pattern of farm work changed. Other trades were also affected; many blacksmiths went out of business, whereas firms selling agricultural machinery flourished.

The most exciting invention of our time has been that of the computer which is now creating a real revolution in many jobs, causing such radical change that some people are calling this period the Second Industrial Revolution. Tasks such as filing, letter-writing, industrial design, information retrieval and calculations can all be accomplished with precision and speed. This is likely to affect all jobs in the future, either directly or indirectly, so that schools and colleges are training as many young people as possible to become familiar with computers.

Economic and Political Trends

The economic and political climate of a nation influences the general level of wealth and employment, but its effects are subtle and complex and even experts do not agree as to their causes and significance. Broadly speaking, however, we can say that a Labour Government in power tends to encourage state-run industry and trades unions, and a Conservative Government to support private enterprise. When a Labour Government was in office from 1945-1951, for instance, all railway and certain bus and haulage companies were nationalized. Obviously, these changes produced significant differences for the employees involved. Each railway company had previously kept its own rules, uniform, rates of pay, systems of training,

▲
1 In 1931 two thirds of the men in Jarrow, a town in north eastern England, had no work. They marched to London in angry and bitter protest.

and so on, whereas when British Rail was formed, methods of operation and wages became standard throughout the country.

National economy goes through phases of affluence and recession. In the 1930s, when this survey begins, Britain was in the grip of a severe depression. The working class had very little money, and it was hard to find employment. Many men and women were put out of work as industry went into a decline. In 1931, the hardships were made even greater when the Means Tests was introduced. Before the state would pay a family any money to live on, the members were subjected to ruthless and humiliating investigations, forced to raise money in any way they could by selling their possessions and begging from their relatives. The gap between the rich and the poor was a very great one.

After the tough years of the 1930s, the Second World War brought far-reaching changes. Many firms had to close, or to alter the kinds of goods they made or the services they offered. Volunteers were brought in to help run businesses. Air-raid emergencies, shortages of goods and Government control over manufacture, fuel and conscription meant that working life was full of uncertainty. It could be exciting, frustrating, tense and rewarding by turns.

The post-war period was one of growing affluence, and throughout the 1950s and '60s work was easy to find. Wages improved in relation to the cost of living, so that most families became comparatively better-off. From the 1970s onwards, the trend has reversed and has been towards higher prices and wages which do not keep pace with inflation. Unemployment, of course, is a problem which has grown again.

One natural effect of these cycles is that when work is easy to come by and wages are good, then people will be more fussy about the jobs they take up, and apt to change employers if they are not satisfied. When work is in short supply, then a job can seem the most desirable thing in the world, and people are more likely to stick to whatever employment they can find and try to make a success of it. In short, the economic state of the country will affect the attitudes and efforts of the people in work, and in times of hardship give even the lowest-paid jobs a prestige and an attractiveness which they lose in more affluent times.

Workforce

The type of people who make up the workforce varies over the years. In the 1930s, the majority of children went to work at the age of 14, whereas today nobody under the age of 16 is allowed to leave school and take up full-time employment. The greatest change in the last fifty years has been the growing number of women who are in work. Many women worked during the war, often called-up by the Government to do so if they had no young children, and after the war the habit was never quite lost! There was a temporary lull in the 1950s, when many chose to return to a quiet domestic life, but since then more and more women have taken on jobs and careers. In the 1950s and early '60s most unmarried women worked, and gradually those with no children, or with grown-up children, joined them. During the 1970s and the present time it has become more usual for mothers with small or school-age children to work. In some cases this is from economic necessity, particularly in the last five or six years, when the wage of a lower-paid worker is scarcely enough to support a family and needs to be supplemented by a second person's earnings. In other cases women find that they are reluctant to abandon a promising career when they have children and they try to keep in full or part-time work.

Laws

Laws regarding employment result from a need to establish certain working conditions which must be adhered to on grounds of safety, fair pay, reasonable terms of service, protection of individual rights, and so on. They set up a framework which affects all jobs and the way they are carried out. For example, looking once again at the issue of working women, it can be seen that it was once often difficult for them to keep a job or to obtain fair pay. Legislation has been introduced over the last fifteen years which compels employers to pay them equal rates with men, and to keep a job open for a woman for several months when she needs to stay at home to have a baby. It can be a legal offence to refuse a female applicant for a job simply because she is a woman. Laws are never perfect, and there are always loopholes which can be

▲
2   A staff agency of 1953. This woman is being interviewed for a job as a nursemaid.

today receive at least two weeks holiday and many as much as four or five weeks. Due to the present shortage of work, it has been suggested that a three- or four-day working week may become common in the future.

*The expectation of a life at work. . .should be changed to life, with leisure and work taking equal priorities. In truth, the prospect of a full lifetime working is a depressing one given the unpleasantness of most jobs. . . . (*The Collapse of Work, Clive Jenkins and Barry Sherman, Methuen, 1979*).*

exploited by employer and employee, but they are passed in an attempt to ensure decent and humane working conditions for the population. Some of the more important statutes are included in the Date List at the end of the book.

We will now look at some of the more general changes in the pattern of working life. Some of these changes have been brought about by legislation, while others are the result of customs which have gradually altered over the years. Very often trades unions have helped to effect these changes by negotiating new conditions of service with management, often through peaceful discussion but sometimes through provoking strikes and industrial disruption.

Hours and Holidays

In the 1930s it was common for most workers to be employed five and a half or six days a week, putting in ten or eleven hours each day. The average holiday would be one or two weeks off a year. Since the war, the eight-hour working day has become normal, with more generous lunch and coffee breaks. Many employees choose to put in overtime hours, however, which are usually paid at a higher rate. All full-time workers

Hiring Staff

Newspaper advertisements have always been a good way of finding work. Many people find jobs through personal connections, too, but this was probably of greater importance in the pre-war period. Nowadays most employers are looking first for qualifications, whether they are at CSE or degree level. Even for the simplest job, CSE passes can convince the employer that the candidate has the keenness and interest in work that is looked for. Apprenticeships, whereby young people were set to learn a trade over a period of several years, earning little money until they had mastered the skills required, are less common today and it is often expected now that the young person will have had some prior practical or vocational training at school or college.

Many people now find work, especially temporary work, through employment agencies. In the 1930s, these agencies usually existed to provide families with servants and nannies, but after the war fewer people were willing to go into service. Eventually, in the 1960s, agencies took on a new lease of life, offering to supply firms with office staff, lorry drivers, shop assistants and so on. The old-fashioned Government "employment exchanges" have followed the trend,

3   A modern Job Centre, run by the Government.

▲ 4   Bygone festivities, as a team from Sainsbury's dressed up for the Colchester carnival in 1939.

5   Many firms have always tried to provide good facilities for their employees. Here is a staff canteen of the 1930s.

▼

◀ 6   A Personnel Officer talks to a young store assistant.

Social Life

The social life offered by a company varies very much from firm to firm, and even within one company it can change a great deal over the years. Some firms recall that the pre-war years were a golden age for staff outings, social clubs, cricket teams, debates, theatrical productions and so on. Others find that they can arouse more enthusiasm today than ever before for Family Days, staff competitions and team sports. The staff outing is perhaps the recreation most popular in the earlier days, and least likely to be found today. The outing was often conducted on an annual basis, and the entire workforce of a factory, shop or office would take to a hired train or fleet of buses and set off to the seaside or to a favourite picnic spot for the day.

Welfare

Before the 1950s, when state benefits were very limited, many firms provided special funds to help out employees with sickness pay and pensions. Nowadays, all workers have entitlement to benefits from the Government which ensures that they can support their families, whatever happens. This is funded by the National Insurance Contributions which are paid by employers and employees. Some firms, however, continue to offer their staff voluntary pension schemes and health plans which can give special advantages.

Staff welfare has become a specialized part of a firm's operation over the last twenty years or so. Employees used to take their problems to their department manager, or perhaps even to the boss himself, especially in family-run firms. Today, most shops, companies and factories of any size will have a full-time Personnel Officer whose job it is to help hire staff, to see that they are trained, and to deal with any problems that may arise during their employment.

giving way to stylish "Job Centres" where those looking for work can see lists of vacancies displayed and consult a member of staff personally about employment problems.

Wages

As we have seen, wages improve or decline in general terms according to the national economy. Individual occupations can become better or worse paid within this framework, as every employee knows. The following list gives a rough guide as to how wages have changed over the years due to the altered value of money:

Average Weekly Wage (not including bonuses, overtime, etc)

	1930s	1980s
Pottery worker	£2.50	£140
Brewery worker	£1.05	£80-£90
Biscuit packer	£0.50	£54-£65
Sewing work	£1.25	£44
Farm labourer	£2.50	£84
Shop assistant	£0.52½	£60
Typist	£1.00	£75

11

2
Shops

The work of shop assistants has changed over the last fifty years, just as the shops themselves have altered. Department stores and small family-owned shops declined in popularity after the war, to be replaced mainly by chain stores and supermarkets, with a shift from the notion of "customer service" to the "self-selection" principle. Before the 1950s, the assistant would serve a customer with everything she wanted to buy; later, when many stores placed their goods on display for the customer to choose without help, the work of the shop assistant became, in general, less skilled.

Training in the 1930s

A school-leaver of the 1930s would regard the job of sales assistant as a proper trade, and would probably expect to stay with the same store for years, gradually working his or her way up through the hierarchy. Much was expected of the young trainee, but much was promised; applicants were encouraged by advertising slogans such as: "All managers chosen from counter staff" (Sainsbury's 1937) and the young man or woman could expect, in time, to become not merely a shop assistant, but a skilled grocer, draper,

7   An advertisement of 1937 gives details of pay ▶ and benefits offered to young men looking for a job in the grocery trade.

12

▲
8   Here the new trainees are learning the precise way to cut a cheese.

butcher, and so on. In the grocery trade, for instance, very little food was pre-packed, and the new assistant would be trained in the arts of blending teas of different strengths, judging the quality of barrels of butter and sides of bacon, and cutting whole cheeses into neat pieces of correct weight.

An employer looking for a ready-trained salesman in the soft furnishing department would choose an applicant only if he had a high degree of competence. A handbook of the day suggests that he should be tested by such questions as: "Describe the fabrics (and state where they may be obtained) which you would suggest using for curtains for (a) A Louis XVI bedroom (b) An Adam dining room (c) A Chippendale lounge". (*The Furnishing Soft Goods Department*, W. A. Gibson Martin, 1937). What is more, once employed, the salesman would be required to increase his knowledge by touring factories to see how the fabrics were actually produced and printed. The guide suggests that the employee will be happy to give up a few days of his annual holiday to do this!

Staff Conduct and Welfare

Staff treated customers with a respect and deference that we might find overwhelming today. Selling had to be courteous, with all customers addressed as "Sir" or "Madam",

9   Style and graciousness were the essence of pre-war department stores. The staff were expected to give attentive yet unhurried service.
▼

10 Notice the smart uniform and appearance of this young lift attendant.

and yet the assistant was expected to be persuasive and encourage the customer to buy, without being aggressive or pushy. In many stores the staff had to keep to strict rules of dress, wearing navy or black without jewellery or accessories. Conduct, too, was regulated;

14

a staff guide for 1934 (Kendal Milne and Co) cautions employees to "be careful to avoid standing in groups, calling loudly across the Departments, walking arm-in-arm. . .and otherwise creating an atmosphere of carelessness and inefficiency".

In certain large stores "the boss" operated a reign of terror, ensuring proper behaviour from his staff by prowling through the departments, ready to pounce if there was a missing price ticket, a shoddy display or a day-dreaming assistant. One grocery manager was known to sweep the entire array of goods off the counter with his stick if he did not like the way they were arranged!

Loyalty was expected from the staff, and in many shops was repaid with personal care and attention from the management. Mr Bentall of Bentall's Department Store, Kingston-upon-Thames, used to put a note in the pay packets of his staff, asking them to come and see him if they were in any sort of trouble. Like other good-hearted bosses, he would make up wages when staff were ill, and even paid for the family to have a holiday when convalescence was needed.

It is understandable that many people were eager to accept the security of a job in a large store, especially during the unemployment problems of the 1930s. An assistant could feel part of a team and have a satisfying sense of making a real contribution to the firm. To have this security, a high level of commitment had to be made, which meant giving up certain personal freedoms, even in private life. Some stores insisted that employees asked permission before they became engaged to be married. Others expected all unmarried workers to live in hostels and obey strict rules concerning bedtimes, meals, visitors and so on. Despite the restrictions, however, living in a hostel could be friendly and relaxed, with the company of others, meals provided, and often pleasant recreational activities with tennis courts, gardens and pianos all at hand. Even married staff were expected to give their primary loyalty to the firm: "You had very little

private life, and your family expected you when they saw you." (Store assistant).

The Small Shop

A girl or boy starting a career in a small local shop might find the job more informal and varied. In the 1930s, a young girl of 14 started work in a northern pawnbroker's. Typically, for the times, her wages were 10s 6d (52½p) per week and she worked on average from 8 am till 7 pm each day, with Sunday and one half-day off. But she recalls that she "enjoyed every minute of it". The conditions were hard, with "no heating, flag floors, and red noses all round!" Indeed, many shops were completely unheated until the late 1930s or '40s. "And yet, it was great — there was more humour and fun."

On Saturday nights the streets were full of people as the shops stayed open until at least 9 pm, and the young assistants enjoyed the lively atmosphere as the butchers and greengrocers tried to sell off most of their wares. Often the prices would be reduced dramatically, partly because people had little money to spare, and partly because there was no electric refrigeration to preserve the food till Monday. Provisions were usually kept cool by huge blocks of ice which the assistants had to drag inside as they were delivered.

War-Time

When the war came, in 1939, many of the male staff in shops were called up, and women took over their positions, doing jobs they had never done before, such as driving delivery vans. Previously, the retail trade had been dominated by men, but after the war the women stayed on and outnumbered the men. An assistant's duties in the war years might include fire-watching from the roof of the shop at night, or organizing the staff bread ration. The traders were hit badly, as most foodstuffs, and many other products such as clothes, were rationed during the war. It did not matter how much money a

▲
11   In the war, shop assistants such as these found themselves selling gas masks and first aid packs to the public.

customer had; if she had used up her meagre ration of coupons, she could buy no more meat, butter, eggs or sugar.

Shop assistants learnt to be adaptable, alert, and responsible. Assistants who had specialized in selling high-class gentlemen's outfits might now be called upon to sell gas masks and black-out material! Others had to know how to usher customers to air raid shelters when the sirens sounded, and all had to be willing to turn out in the night to clear up the mess if the shop suffered bomb damage.

When the war ended, many firms were willing to take their former employees back again on their return from the army. Re-training schemes were offered, and one has the impression that shops tried hard to find suitable new jobs for those who had gone away, taking into account that many had

left as raw, inexperienced youths, and had come back as responsible adults.

The Post-War Era: New Patterns in Shopping

Several factors led to the rise of the chain store and supermarket from the 1950s onwards. The economy improved, and people were earning more money; they wanted to choose freely from the greatly-expanded range of products available, often making "impulse buys". Money was more abundant, but time was tighter; there were fewer "gentlemen of leisure" and more women working who now had to fit in their shopping when they could. In short, the public was eager to buy, susceptible to the latest fashions, but keen to snap up their purchases as fast as they could. Shops which laid out goods so that the customers could help themselves were the obvious answer. Additionally, much of the impeccable service of the department stores had been aimed at high-class clientele, and now that the working classes too had money to spend, much of the "genteel" atmosphere dissolved, and assistants began to treat customers as equals. Rules and regulations regarding dress, conduct and procedure were relaxed.

Supermarkets

In 1947 there were only ten supermarkets in Britain, but by 1961 the number had risen to 750 and was increasing rapidly. The idea had originated in the USA, and was introduced cautiously in Britain, but soon caught on. The "help yourself" approach was made possible by new electric refrigeration, which meant that chilled and frozen foods could be laid out in open cabinets for inspection, and by methods of pre-packing, which allowed

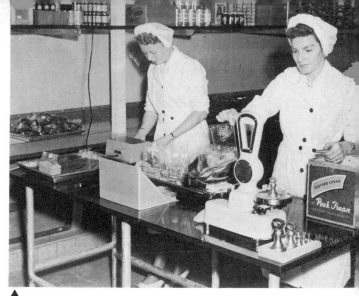

▲
12 When goods were first pre-packed, they would often arrive in loose quantities at the store, where staff would make them up into individual packs. Here women are shown weighing up biscuits behind the scenes. (Probably early 1950s).

13 This picture, taken in 1952, shows a typical small grocer's of the period. Note the unprotected display of meat pies, faggots and crumpets, which would not be allowed today!
▼

14 A modern supermarket showing cashiers at work.

goods such as butter, biscuits, cheese and sugar to be put out ready for sale.

Inevitably, many of the skills of selling were lost. The shop assistant was no longer required to know the quality of bacon or the blend of a tea. In supermarkets, jobs now fell into two categories, those of cashiers who added up all the customer's purchases and took the money for them, and those of shelf-fillers who replaced the goods that were taken off the shelves. The woman who started work in the pawnbroker's as a girl worked in a grocery store that went self-service in 1962, and found it "not as satis-fying as serving a person all the way round".

Boutiques

In the 1960s, however, a new type of shop emerged which provided young people with a sales job quite different from the trad-itional type of employment. Cheap, ready-made and fashionable clothes were in great demand and plenty of shops — often known as "boutiques" — opened to cater for the trend. Assistants could dress as exotically as they liked — indeed, they would not be con-sidered for the job if they turned up in the sober hues expected of the previous gene-ration! Pop or rock music was generally played non-stop, and for those who liked the noise, the bustle, and the colourful fashions, the work offered an interesting opportunity and was often paid reasonably well into the bargain.

The fashion stores have remained with us since then, although many are now branches of national firms rather than being in-dividually owned. Much of the excitement of the "swinging sixties" wore off in the 1970s, and it became apparent that being a fashion assistant today can be a very dead-end job. Staff are no longer required to know about types of fabric or how to pin clothes for alteration; customers begin to consider them a nuisance, rather than a help, if they offer to help with selecting or fitting of garments.

Working in a Shop Today

The image of a shop or supermarket assistant in the 1960s and '70s, therefore, became one of a lethargic, unfriendly creature, uninterested in customers and ready to pack in the job at a moment's notice. "Some of them are thinking about where they were last night, or where they're going to be tonight. They don't seem to be living for the moment." Of course, this is a generalization, and many stores retained high standards of staff training and conduct. But it is certainly true that much of the work became less skilled and more monotonous during this period.

In the last few years, though, unemployment has once again begun to bite, and shops usually have many applicants for each job. This has meant more careful selection, and personnel managers are looking for employees who show enthusiasm and willingness for the work. This is likely to improve the status of shop work as the staff themselves become more committed to it.

Conditions, of course, are much improved nowadays, and shops are required by law to be adequately ventilated and heated. An eight-hour day is now normal, and most large stores provide good staff facilities such as canteens. Wages, which rose relatively fast in the 1960s and early '70s, have perhaps fallen behind again though; a trainee in a supermarket can be paid as little as £50 basic per week today.

Although, as we have seen, the work of a shop assistant no longer necessarily involves lengthy training, there are still many shops where the staff are required to be knowledgeable and skilful. To be a butcher, a seller of electrical equipment or of carpets, for instance, needs considerable skill or knowledge. Many shops organize training sessions once a week for their assistants. New equipment, too, such as sophisticated electronic tills which are linked into a computer, mean that the staff must be trained to use them accurately and unhesitatingly.

The qualities looked for in an assistant of the 1930s were eagerness, honesty, endurance, plus a deep respect for authority and humility in the presence of superiors and customers. Today's assistants are still required to be honest; a supermarket cashier, for instance, handles enormous sums of money. The best ones are still cheerful and polite; however, humility and respect are less important than firmness in some situations. A large supermarket or chain store can be quite an aggressive environment to work in, and the kind of staff wanted are those who can "hold their own with customers". (Personnel Manager).

3
Factories

The 1930s heralded a new era for manufacturing. There was a revolution in the design of factories, giving priority to space, lighting and safe working conditions. The old image of a factory was that of a sooty, dreary building, perhaps many storeys high, with awkward stairs and passages. In the 1930s the opportunity arose for many new factories to be built, because electricity became widely available to industry, and firms could now locate their premises in areas far away from coal fields. Often they chose sites on city outskirts, close to main roads for ease of transport. The new designs were mainly for buildings of only one or two storeys, for greater convenience, with no permanent dividing walls inside so that the layout could be adapted easily to different needs.

However, not all firms could adopt such standards straightaway. One food factory which made pies and sausages is remembered as being unheated and unpleasantly unhygienic. Cleaning took place only once a week, by which time the grease was an inch thick on the floor. All the staff were relieved when new premises were found in 1939, complete with new equipment chosen for greater safety and ease of cleaning.

War-Time

During the war, far more women came to work in the factories, often helping to make munitions or essential military equipment, such as parachutes. Many private factories found that their space was requisitioned by the Government and that they were put out of business till after the war. Those that were able to stay in business had to "blackout" the premises so that no lights showed at night, and organize fire-watching teams who kept on the alert in case bombs were dropped. Many employees slept on the premises on nights when it was difficult to get transport home.

Post-War Automation

After the war, the trend towards greater automation increased. Factory owners have always tried to install equipment which would enable jobs to be done faster and with less human aid, but the last thirty years have seen great advances in this respect. In the 1930s, for instance, girls were employed to put the cream fillings into biscuits by hand, and even to match up two halves of the biscuit to make sure they were of the same colour! Later, this was no longer necessary; machines could fill the biscuits, and baking ovens became more efficient so that the biscuits were uniform in colour.

Conveyor belts had been introduced before the war, but in the 1950s far greater use was made of them. Car factories showed

▲ 15   The old factory of Wedgwood, built close to the canal so that pottery could be taken away by barge. Notice the smoky atmosphere!

16   In contrast, the new Wedgwood factory built in the 1930s is low in height, clean and light, and set in landscaped surroundings.
▼

17   In this factory meat products were made, and the photo, taken around the 1940s period, shows conditions that were good for the time. There is plenty of space and the area is well-lit. Safety was considered, for there is a fire extinguisher visible.

18   Women working to make ammunition during the war.

▲
19   This photo shows the comparative lack of automation in the 1930s and '40s. There are no conveyor belts and the chocolate boxes are being filled, wrapped and stacked by hand.

an extreme example of the use of belts in their production lines. Supervisors would try to get more and more work out of their men by speeding up the conveyor belts. Sometimes the supervisor would start the line moving at a reasonable speed and then gradually accelerate it. Workers recall that such speeds could be intolerable, especially for older men. Such practices have now been ruled out, but they added to the discontent of workers in many industries and contributed to the grievances between workers and management which have come to a head in the last twenty years, often resulting in strikes.

Managers and Employees

The manufacturing industry has always been known for having a wide division between management and workers. Some people consider that this gap has grown worse in the 1970s and '80s. One reason may be that the head of department used to be a person who had worked his or her way up right from the humblest job and knew the work thoroughly. Nowadays many people are trained for management at colleges and universities and don't have the basic experience. "They look at the figures and the quality control, but they're not technically minded — if something goes wrong they still have to rely on the tradesmen [production workers] to put the fault right." (Senior mould-maker at a pottery firm). Today a worker might still enter management, but probably in the job of a "foreman", who is responsible for overseeing a team of workers, but who is not involved in office work or production strategy. Foremen sometimes find themselves in an uneasy position as they are now set apart from their workmates: "They can no longer be familiar with the blokes — they've got to dish out the discipline, got to change sides." (Brewery Personnel Manager).

Job Satisfaction

The problem of boredom in factory life has always been acute, since repetitive and noisy work is involved. Workers often say that they deliberately make their minds go blank so that they can simply get through the hours of the day. Clock-watching, absenteeism and personal frustration are the inevitable consequences of such stress. In some factories even the physical elements of the tasks have been removed; now that machinery is more advanced, men and women are employed as "machine-minders" who stand and watch the progress of production and simply correct any mistake that the machine makes, such as putting double caps on a bottle. Obviously, some people find such work more dreary than others. One manager considers that women have a better tolerance of it because "they can stand monotony better than men". It is unlikely that the majority of women would agree with this judgement!

Recently, certain attempts have been made to re-think the whole business of factory employment, in order to increase job satisfaction. One major advance has been the introduction of "Quality Circles", at present limited to a few companies in Great Britain, but already enjoying great success. This is a scheme whereby a group of employees from each department forms a Circle with the purpose of improving working conditions and production. They choose a name for their Circle, such as the "Solvits", and meet for an hour a week in the firm's time. The idea is based on the principle that a member of the workforce is not merely a "pair of hands" but in fact has "managerial" experience in his or her own life — as a woman is "manager" of her household, for instance. Such experience and ability can be used at work if the right opportunities are given. The Quality Circles look at particular problems in their departments, and make suggestions for improvements, often carrying out lengthy research programmes to back up their ideas. The management undertakes to implement the schemes if they are valid, and the workers have the satisfaction of contributing to the firm and of putting their bright ideas into practice. Even long-standing and major technical problems have been solved by the resourcefulness of Quality Circles.

Health and Safety

Legislation over the years has helped to make factories safer and more pleasant places to work. For instance, in 1937 it became compulsory to provide fresh drinking water and in 1961 safety restrictions were put on the use of dangerous machinery. Factory Inspectors have the duty of making sure that premises come up to standard, but throughout the period there has been the problem of employers evading the law, and of there being too few Inspectors to enforce it. In 1931 the report of the Chief Inspector of Factories said that there was evidence of illegal employment, with boys working 74 hours a week, when in fact the hours of "young persons" had been controlled by law for many years. And in the weaving mills, it was discovered that women were prone to develop cancer of the mouth because of the harmful oil placed in the "kissing shuttles" which the women would thread by placing them in their mouths. Although self-threading shuttles were introduced just before the 1930s, the women could work faster the old way, and since they were on "piece-work" they continued to use that way, unless they knew an Inspector was coming.

Many health hazards have been dealt with, but it is likely that new ones will constantly be created or discovered. For example, when artificial silk became popular in the 1940s it was found that workers could be poisoned by the fibres. In the last ten years we have had the discovery that asbestos causes serious problems for those coming into close contact with it. There are always hidden dangers in manufacturing occupations, the consequences of which may not be noticed for many years.

Obvious health risks, such as excess noise, can be dealt with more easily. Nowadays workers in very noisy conditions are supplied with ear muffs, whereas in earlier times men and women employed in the spinning mills, for instance, often went deaf. Many learnt to lip-read so that they could exchange at least a few words with each other at work, since even those who still had their hearing could not hope to understand what was said with such a din going on.

20   Workers in a spinning mill; the noise of the machinery was intense.

▼

Staff Conditions and Facilities

Most firms provide good facilities for their staff nowadays, and certainly factories built since the 1930s will incorporate such features as comfortable cloakrooms, staff canteens and even recreational facilities such as TV lounges or billiards rooms. But many old buildings are still in use, and have had little innovation over the last fifty years. It is still possible to visit waste textile mills where the air is filled with dust, the floors are filthy and strewn with debris, and fire risks are high from the likelihood of cigarettes coming into contact with bales of cloth.

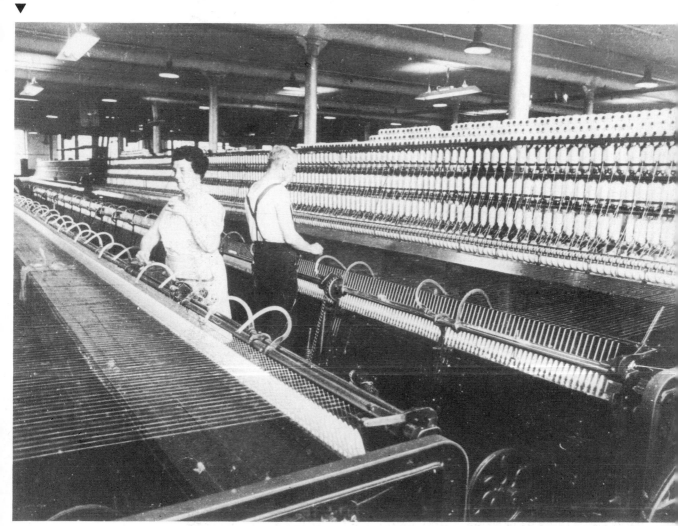

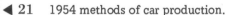
◀ 21 1954 methods of car production.

Facilities for staff can be non-existent except for an outside lavatory and one cold tap. In areas where unemployment is high, men and women will take jobs in these conditions simply because they need the work and there is nowhere else they can find it. This is an extreme example of factory work, but nevertheless even the official Inspectors find that there is much of concern in the manufacturing industry:

Many people still have to spend virtually their whole working lives in poorly-lit premises, with dirty walls and cramped and poorly ventilated conditions, which are a daily affront to the human spirit even if they present little actual risk to their physical well being. (Inspector's report 1970).

Changes in Processes and Goods Produced

If we look at the post-war history of factories, it becomes plain that the kinds of goods produced and processes involved have altered. Spinning and weaving, once a major industry of northern England, have declined dramatically since the war, whereas factories producing food — canned, packed, frozen, etc — have expanded. All these changes affect the types of jobs available.

Internal changes within a factory, too, can alter work patterns. One example can be given of a particular brewery in Tiverton, Devon, a branch of a national company, where many local men were employed until 1982. In the 1930s the job used to involve plenty of physical work. Hops arrived in big "pockets" and were emptied out and weighed. Malt was loaded up and moved to the place where it was ground up and mashed, then shovelled out again. In the last twenty years, hop oil was introduced, which could be circulated by pipes. More auto-

22 The contrast of the latest methods in car manufacture, showing workers with ear muffs for protection and control panels which conduct much of the operation automatically.
▼

26

mation was brought in, so that only a control panel was needed to send the malt through the various stages of brewing. However, even this did not bring the high standards of production that the company sought, and in 1982 the brewery was closed as new "push-button" plants had been built elsewhere, each of which could do the work of several smaller breweries.

Computer control is being introduced into many factories now, and some use "robots" to do assembly tasks which were once human jobs. Although many people are apprehensive of this change, fearing that it will put more and more men and women out of a job, these innovations are surely releasing many from the very tedious and wearying work which is more suitable to be done by machines than humans. The worry is, of course, that there will not be enough jobs of other kinds for all the members of the population who want to work. It can only be hoped that this is an awkward transition period, and that newer and better kinds of work will be generated in the near future for those who find that the "micro-chip" has made them redundant.

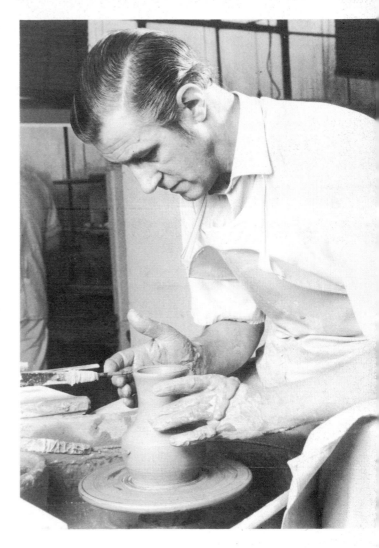

23   Some industries still retain an element of ▶ craftsmanship. Here is a modern potter, working in a factory where hand-throwing is still needed for the best quality pieces.

4
Transport

Transport is the means of conveying passengers or goods from one place to another. Throughout the period from the 1930s, the transport business has been very important to the national economy, and the trend towards giving faster services over longer distances has affected the jobs of transport workers. High-speed passenger trains, international air flights and juggernaut lorries are all commonplace today, but were almost unknown in the 1930s. Trains, road vehicles and planes have all been modernized, resulting in easier handling for their drivers or pilots. Some of the adventure of driving steam trains or of flying to the Far East has gone, but hours and conditions of work are generally better, and the work is safer today.

Trains

In the 1930s, railways were still privately owned, and a youngster would join one of the several companies, such as the Great Western Railway, straight from school. He would usually start as a cleaner; he would be measured to see if he was tall enough, given a second-hand set of overalls, and then sent off in a "gang" of five or six lads to clean up the engines as they returned from duty. It was a hard, sweaty job, as all the oil and grease had to be removed; a layer of grease built up on the overalls which protected the wearer from burns or scalds from the sparks or the boiling water. Overalls were never washed — only burnt when they wore out!

Next, the young man might be promoted to rank of fireman, and he would now be "on the road", tending and stoking the engine as the train sped on its way. The fire had to be fuelled little and often, the level of water in the boiler kept constant, and the store of coal dampened to eliminate dust. Every engine needed different handling, and thus the fireman's job was highly skilled. The apprentice might only acquire his fireman's badge after he had proved his aptitude by working on over 300 runs. It was a job enjoyed by many:

*As the blast threw the smoke and steam up into the night sky I would keep the steady flow of coal over the half-door, feet astride swinging from left to right, so easy, so wonderful, the ring of the shovel on the fire door, the injector singing softly, the safety valves humming slightly with a full head of steam, the heat, the smell, the crescendo of noise that is the steam engine echoing back from the night stillness of the trees and banks. How wonderful to be an engineman on engines like these. (*Man of the Southern: Jim Evans Looks Back, *Allen and Unwin, 1980).*

A competent fireman could apply to be

trained as a driver, and this training was very exacting. He had to know his routes or "roads" thoroughly, with the speeds required, gradients, signals, stops and so on. He had to be able to locate faults in the engine and make any adjustments needed to keep the train running. This was essential for safety, as steam trains could be very hazardous, the biggest danger being one of "blow-back" in the engine which could send fire out onto the footplate and burn the driver and fireman badly.

Drivers worked their way up from a junior position to that of "top linkman" on long-distance routes. Digs were available if the crew needed to stay away overnight. Some were very grubby and:

It was quite common to get into a warm bed. . . . Many's the time I've woken up with a complete stranger besides me. (Men of the Great Western, *Peter Grafton, Allen and Unwin, 1979*).

It was important that a fireman and a driver got along together. Quarrels could easily turn into wars! The fireman might accuse the driver of working the engine too hard, or the driver call the fireman lazy. They might even fall out over their dinner — arguing as to whether kippers or bacon should be fried first in the shovel over the fire! Many firemen and drivers got on well together, and tried to keep together as a team. Although they had to keep strictly to a timetable, there were times when the run was leisurely and railwaymen recall such pleasures as stopping to pick primroses, or to buy their eggs and vegetables from stationmasters along the way!

Many stationmasters had little work to do in country stations where passengers might number as few as two or three a week. They kept pigs, hens, and gardened enthusiastically

24   Driver and fireman on board an old steam train, one of the Bristol to Paddington express trains (1934).
▼

in-between trains. A signalman was a "creature apart" up in his box, and it used to be said: "If you are unmarried when you take over a box, chances are you will never marry." Until the 1950s the signalboxes had no electricity or even gas to heat or light them. Working in signals was preferred by some, as it was cleaner than being with engines, but it was a lonelier job.

The age of steam lasted till the late 1950s and during these years there were changes, of course. The companies in the 1930s were strict employers, often harsh with discipline and intolerant of complaints from their workers. But they paid fairly well, and often

helped with housing for their men. Railwaymen were proud of their work and had good status. But in the late 1940s much of this prestige vanished and wages no longer compared so favourably with those of other manual workers. In 1947 the railways were nationalized, and British Rail, a public corporation, became responsible for running the nation's railways.

In the 1950s the first diesel and electric trains were introduced. Drivers could apply to retrain as "motormen", and after six weeks or so they could emerge ready to drive the efficient, quiet and clean engines. Because the new trains were more reliable in operation, the runs became less adventurous and the work easier. One driver found that life became less interesting, but that the

25   A modern train cab with easy controls and a comfortable seat.

▼

change was not without its consolations; he was put on boat-train runs in the southeast and found the pleasures of the beach and fishing a great attraction in-between the outward and return journeys.

Newcomers to the railway today still need to spend months or even years learning their skill as drivers, but drivers no longer have to look after the train when they come off duty, as they used to in the days of steam. Signalmen need to be as responsible and alert as they ever were, but modernized controls and safety mechanisms have reduced the risk of accidents resulting from human error. Indeed, the railway safety record has improved beyond all recognition in the last twenty years, and fatal accidents on the railways are now extremely rare.

Acquiring a job on the railway is now exceedingly difficult. Stringent economies are being practised in an attempt to keep the railways viable financially; additionally, there are fewer lines and stations to service now, since the Beeching Report of 1963 recommended the closure of many branch lines. Relationships between the men themselves, and with their employers are generally easier today in terms of better communication and equality — although there are still major differences of opinion, as the 1982 railway strikes showed! Hierarchy is less important: "The days when one man went to London (as a driver) and looked down on the man not permitted to go beyond Brockenhurst were now out," recalled Jim Evans (*Man of the Southern*), as he contemplated the changes that had taken place in the transition from the mysterious, sooty, magic world of steam to the safe, clean and cost-conscious rail industry of today.

Road Transport

In the 1930s there was a variety of vehicles on the road being used for goods transport — horse-drawn carts and vans, lorries, and bicycles. The day of the horse was, of course, fast ending, but before the war men were still needed who could care for horses, turn them out to a high standard, and drive them safely through the ever-increasing traffic on city streets.

There was plenty of work in the delivery business, whether by horse or by motor. Many shops still delivered regularly to customers, kitting their delivery men out in smart livery; and there were short trips to collect goods from railway stations and docks. Until about twenty years ago, many products were sent packed in straw and wooden crates. A lorry driver delivering bleach, for instance, would have glass bottles in crates. Not only would they weigh heavy, but he would be expected to stop often, calling at many small shops, to unload a crate or two for an order. Nowadays a firm is likely to refuse an order of less than 70 cases, which will be unloaded by warehousemen at a wholesaler's or supermarket depot. The bleach will be in plastic bottles packed in cardboard boxes, and the whole lot will be stacked on pallets (flat wooden frames) and loaded and unloaded by fork-lift truck. The driver may still have to know how to "rope-up" a load, but does less heavy lifting and loading.

In the early days, lorries were a great labour to drive, as they were heavy, noisy and cumbersome, and were only allowed by law to go at 20 mph. There were no motorways, and long-distance trips could take several days, especially in bad weather. The opening of the motorways from the 1960s on, and the creation of city bypasses, have made the lorry driver's job easier and more pleasant. The modern lorry is capable of greater speed, faster braking, and is — on the whole — quieter. Some are very well-equipped, with bunks for sleeping, and many drivers today use Citizen's Band radio which enables them to chat to other drivers on the road and summon help quickly if they have a breakdown.

Safety has always been of vital importance, and over the years legislation has been introduced to prevent overloading, excessive hours

AWARDED FIRST PRIZE AT REGENTS PARK
HORSE SHOW, JUNE 9TH 1930.

worked, and to ensure that vehicle maintenance is adequate and that strict records are kept. In 1930 the hours that a driver might spend at the wheel were reduced to 11. In recent years legislation has gradually become tighter till the length of time spent at the wheel in any one day or week is strictly controlled. In general a driver must not exceed 4 hours on the road at a stretch, and altogether in a day he must not drive for more than 8 hours. A special Heavy

▲
Three generations of Sainsbury's road transport:
26 This first shows a prize-winning turn-out for the Regents Park Horse Show in 1930.

Goods Vehicle Licence is needed before a driver can take a lorry on the road. Since 1968 the standards for hauliers (those who operate a lorry service, either as an owner-driver or by owning a fleet of vehicles) have been raised, and professional exams must be passed to show that the person is competent.

27   The second shows a lorry of 1955. The driver
is collecting eggs from the farm in wooden crates,
which would be sold in the shops later.

28   A modern heavy goods lorry. The driver is
trying his skill in the Sainsbury's "Driver of the
Year" competition.

29   In the 1940s, cabin crew were expected to attend passengers as if they were in the role of personal butler.

Subjects included in the courses leading to these exams are law (as related to transport), accounts, industrial relations, and technical standards of equipment and maintenance. Many lorry drivers prefer to be owner-drivers if possible, and be their own bosses. Lorry drivers have been called "a special breed of men", and have always been known as independent and individual in their approach to work.

Planes

Long-distance air travel was exciting and challenging in the 1930s. There were no jet planes until the 1950s; aeroplanes flew lower and slower. A typical trip from Australia to England took ten days, stopping over-night. At this time the airlines were catering mainly for colonial government employees and the very rich, for fares were high; their attitude was that their customers should have the best of everything on their flight. They attempted to create aeroplanes which were more like hotels, and provided attentive cabin staff who acted like personal butlers to their passengers. The staff (only men at this period) served high-class food and drink and even saw their passengers safely into bed at night on certain aircraft equipped with bunks!

Usually, though, overnight stops were

34

made, partly because the pilot could not fly safely at night due to lack of proper airport lighting. Crew and passengers ate and slept at the same hotels, and the dinners were conducted rather like those on an elegant cruise. Food poisoning could be a serious problem, however, because local kitchens and foodstuffs were sometimes contaminated. It could be very dangerous if the captain and crew were all smitten at the same time while flying. Later, in the 1950s, when frozen foods were introduced, meals could be prepared at the airlines' own kitchens, situated at the airports or at a ground base; they could then be loaded onto the aircraft and heated up when necessary during the flight. Nowadays, as a double check, all the crew eat different food from each other.

In the 1940s, air hostesses arrived, much to the horror of the pilots' wives! Some wrote in to protest, claiming that their husbands would be stolen from them! The first air hostesses were often brought in as trained nurses in uniform and expected to deal chiefly with cases of air sickness, which were more common then, because of bumpy flying. They were also expected to reassure and comfort passengers, and point out to them places of interest as they flew over. As time went on, the stewardesses were allocated more and more passengers to serve, and their main duties merged with those of the male cabin staff, serving food and drink to passengers. Nowadays the cabin crew are regarded more as equals than as servants — indeed, many passengers feel slightly in awe of them!

A job as a pilot has always carried great prestige, but in the early days pilots were badly paid, even though they were seen as heroes by their passengers and used to hand out signed photos as souvenirs. Nowadays pilots are well-paid, and can earn over £30,000 a year. As with drivers, hours of work have been reduced over the years and now a pilot may fly up to 12 hours at a stretch but work only about two weeks of every month.

Great attention had to be paid to improving safety in the 1950s, as there had been many crashes before the war, and the airlines realized that they could only attract passengers if flying could be seen to be safe. All went well until the 1960s, when there were some serious crashes, and there were scandals over the behaviour of pilots on certain airlines, when they were discovered to be reading newspapers or sleeping at times when they should have been awake and active. However, these were obviously extreme examples, and some psychologists blamed crashes more on the strain and boredom of working on the flight deck. A pilot has to be physically fit, and yet remain in cramped conditions during working hours. Further strain has been placed on aircraft crew over the last fifteen years by the rise of hi-jacking incidents, when terrorists or even plain lunatics have tried to take over the aircraft by force.

Today the safety record is good and the work prestigious and well-paid. Many young men and women dream of being pilots or air hostesses and of seeing the world, even though air travel has taken its place as a regular form of transport, rather than being the glamorous and thrilling adventure that it was in the 1930s.

5
Farming

Farming life of the 1930s has for us a nostalgic, picture-book quality. A typical farm would have its herd of cows, each one known by a traditional name, such as Bluebell or Daisy, its flock of chickens clucking around the farmyard, a few pigs rooting in the orchard, and a team of handsome horses to pull the plough. Such farming, where different kinds of animals are kept and varied crops are harvested, is known as mixed farming. Since the 1930s, this has become less and less common and specialization has become more usual, where the farmer concentrates on raising one type of crop or animal.

Although the old-fashioned type of farm sounds ideal, it is important to realize that the 1930s were very lean years, and many farmers had a hard time of it. A farmer now living on the edge of Greater Manchester

30 Horses were essential to farm work before the war. Here the teams are being taken out ready-harnessed to the fields to plough.

▼

recalls that many farmers were desperate to make a living; often the only way they could do so was to move to a farm close to a town, where they could have their own milk round, selling direct to the public.

31   The shepherd; a traditional figure rarely seen today.

▼

Dairies gave no guarantee that they would buy a farmer's milk, and the farmer might have to throw the milk away unless he could turn it into cheese and butter, and even that brought in very little money. British agriculture was in a slump, partly due to cheap imports of grain which flooded the market, making it impossible for British farmers to compete, and partly due to lack of proper Government aid or sensible policies on pricing.

Farming was a labour-intensive occupation at that time, and each farm would have a team of workers. Some of them would have special responsibilities as shepherd, cowman, horseman, and so on. There was then, and still is, a division between the farmers themselves, who own or rent the land which they work, and the farm labourers who are hired by the farmer on a temporary or permanent basis. Many labourers used to live in the farmouse itself and were often expected to be under the farmer's authority day and night. One farmer discovered that his men were disobeying the bed-time hour he had set them and were climbing out of the window to go to the pub! He quickly took action by bricking the window up!

Many extra workers would be brought in at certain seasons, for hay-making, harvesting and potato-picking, for instance. This is still true today, but to a lesser extent; in those days, for example, whole gangs of men would come over from Ireland to help with the hay on farms in the northwest. One Irishman had such a rough crossing that he never dared go back, and he worked on the farm for the rest of his life! Wages were around one shilling (5p) per hour. These periods of intense work were tough, but were

also merry, sociable occasions. Our Manchester farmer remembers those "old days" with fondness:

I remember I enjoyed my young working days so much that at night I'd be thinking — "Only another six or seven hours and I can be getting back to work!"

Horses were an important part of farm life, and this meant that there were jobs for men who knew how to look after them and how to harness and work a team. Using horses to plough, sow and reap was slow but rewarding.

Horses were company for you. They knew their job as much as you did. They were man's friend.

It was strenuous work, walking all day behind the team as it went up and down the field.

Sheep-shearing was done by hand and farmers from neighbouring farms would help each other out in turn. In 1935 Dorothy Hartley wrote:

In mountainous districts, it is still customary to hold large sheepshearing parties in turn at each farm. Usually a barn is cleared, or some sort of shelter put up, straw stacks are thrown down on a clean rick cloth, and there's a regular set-to with beef sandwiches, fresh mustard, cheese, beer, jokes, the news of the district, and some courting. (The Countryman's England).

Developments During and After the War

The war, of course, changed farming, as it did most other occupations. The Government woke up to the fact that farming was of prime importance for the survival of Britain, now that food could not be imported, and farmers were given every encouragement to make the most use of their land. Even shallow hill land was ploughed up in an attempt to grow more of the badly needed oats and corn. "Land Girls" arrived, young and healthy women called-up to help the farmers keep their holdings going at a time when many of the men were sent away to fight. It was a time when necessity proved to be the mother of invention; because there was such pressure to produce food, all sorts of methods were tried out. Sugar beet was introduced as a crop, and farmers learnt how to make sileage as an alternative to hay, as feed for their cattle.

After the war, developments continued, and many farmers started to use tractors which they found could do the work more quickly than the old teams of horses. But for many years tractors and horses were often found together on the same farm. One imagines that when the tractor broke down, the "dratted new machine" would be roundly

◀ 32   A sheep-shearing party of the 1930s.

39

33 Much work was done by hand; here women are seen planting potatoes (1933). Today a machine can do the job.

cursed, and the horses hitched up instead! At the time, oil was reasonable in price and the tractors were a sound economic proposition. Many farmers did well in the war years and in the 1950s.

Work was made easier in other ways; electric milking was introduced, and the traditional milkmaid with stool and pail became a romantic memory from Britain's past! Perhaps the memories of the milkmaids themselves are not quite so romantic

of cold, dark mornings, struggling to hand-milk with numb fingers by the flickering light of a hurricane lamp! Some of the milking procedures were still very old-fashioned by today's standards, however. The farmer might be dependent upon an unreliable generator for his source of electricity and the milk still had to be emptied out of the tank where it collected and poured into churns, which would then be hauled by cart or trailer and placed on a platform outside the farm entrance for collection. Today, all the milk flows into a bulk tank where it is kept cool until the

milk tanker arrives and sucks it out directly. Standards of hygiene have improved beyond recognition over the last fifty years.

The advent of the Milk Marketing Board just before the war meant that farmers were now guaranteed a fixed price for their milk, and could count on making a living from dairy farming.

It was grand — every farmer, whether he was near a town or not, the Milk Marketing Board paid for the milk, one price for everybody. If it weren't for the Board, I don't know where we'd be now. (Manchester farmer).

Modern Farming

In 1949, the number of workers employed in agriculture reached a peak, and since then has declined, dropping to half its former

40

▲

34　The Women's Land Army stepped in to save the harvest in war-time Britain. With many farm workers called up to the armed forces, young women were needed on the land to help food production.

35　Even school playing fields were ploughed up for farming during the war. Notice how horses and a tractor are being used side by side.

▼

▲

36   An early system of electric milking.

37   A modern milking parlour. The working area
is sunken so that the attendant can see to the cows
without having to bend down low.

▼

total in 1969. Agriculture paid its labourers
poorly, and in the post-war years many
young men looked for better money in
towns and factories. Those who stayed had
to learn a new type of farming, with a
mechanized, scientific approach. The war
years had given a spur to research into
farming methods and in the 1950s and '60s
sophisticated new chemicals came into
widespread use in the form of pesticides,
fertilizers and preventative animal medicine.
A farm worker had to keep up with the
latest bewildering array of products from
pharmaceutical companies, which were often
promoted by aggressive selling techniques
and a wealth of persuasive glossy literature.

More and more youngsters from those
who remained in farming went to Agricultural College to learn, since this was the
only way they could study modern, scientific
farming. Although, doubtless, many of them

have received a far wider education this way, the criticism is often made that study from books does not give a young person the same solid grounding in practical farming as would "learning on the job".

Skills of animal husbandry changed, too, in the 1960s and '70s, as intensive and battery farming became more popular. As we have already said, farmers began to specialize, in order to make a living, and this meant that a farm would tend to keep all cattle or all sheep, rather than a few of each. To make the maximum profit, many farmers found that they could keep pigs, or hens, or veal calves permanently indoors, housed in huge, specially constructed buildings with the minimum of space per animal and permanent artificial light — or, in the case of veal calves, permanent darkness. This is known as "battery farming" or "intensive rearing". Obviously, quite a different approach is needed to manage creatures kept in this way, and workers had to learn what injections to give to prevent disease running through the close-quartered animals, how to check battery hens to make sure they laid their proper quota of eggs, and what additives to put in the feeds to promote particular qualities in the meat or eggs. Records and statistics became of importance in assessing the performance of stock, as opposed to the old way of keeping an experienced eye on each individual creature.

In future years we may look back to the 1970s and see it as the period when the trend of super-mechanized, specialized and chemical farming reached its peak. Economic recession and the oil crisis of the early '70s meant that farmers had to think hard about whether they could afford to run bigger or better machines all the time, or to buy such lavish amounts of pesticides, herbicides and fertilizers to sprinkle on their fields. Concern has grown in the last ten years or so about conservation, since there are signs that removing hedges to create huge, windswept fields (easier to manage with modern machinery) and using large quantities of chemicals may be destroying the birds and insects which acted as natural predators against the pests which could spoil a farmer's crops. There are signs that farming is turning again towards a more balanced approach, with less drastic use of powerful chemicals and greater encouragement of natural fertilizers, pesticides and predators.

Farmers have found it difficult, too, to replace and maintain all the modern equipment needed. "Since the tractor came, and complicated machines — that's where the money's gone." (Manchester farmer). This has led to an increase in the number of agricultural contractors, men who own their own equipment — anything from a potato harvester to a tractor and muckspreader — and who will work on a freelance basis for others. The farmer can arrange for a contractor to come in to do a certain job of work, and finds this more economical than buying the machinery to use himself.

Efficient machinery means that fewer and fewer men are needed to work the same amount of land today. Our farmer from Manchester used to work with his family and at least four other men; now, he and his two sons find that there is not really enough work for them all, with 90 cows and a few fields of root crops to look after. At one time, for instance, all the muck and straw had to be cleared out of the cow shed with a hand fork and built into a dung heap; later it would be carted into the fields to be spread over them as manure. Now the dung is free of straw and is swilled away with water into a "slurry tank"; when this is full, the liquid manure can be pumped into a container and sprayed mechanically onto the fields.

Farms have, on the whole, grown bigger in order to be viable. However, the move towards larger, mechanized, specialized units has to some extent been offset over the last decade by an interesting new trend. Many people have been giving up desk and town jobs in order to try their hand at farming, or keeping a smallholding, attracted by the

idea of living in the country and earning their keep, independent of a boss or commercial firm. They welcome the hard physical work spurned by the young men and women of the previous generation, and often do not mind having a lower standard of living in return for the satisfaction of seeing their produce and livestock grow. Plenty of them have found the challenge too much, but many, too, have stayed. They have shown that a holding of up to 20 acres or so *can* support a family today, providing that the costs of labour and equipment are kept down. For, indeed, it is out of the question now for many newcomers to buy a farm of normal size, which would cost more than £400,000 to purchase and stock.

Farming will not return to the days of the

▲
38 Large and expensive pieces of equipment are a feature of farming life today. Many farmers attend demonstrations where they can see the latest machinery being used.

horse and cart, for mechanization is here to stay. However, attitudes towards farming change, and seldom remain at one extreme for long. It is likely that the pendulum is already swinging back, and that we will see farm work once again become more of a craft and an individual skill, less dominated by "factory" attitudes and scientific products, open indeed to new developments, but with a willingness to use them humanely, with due regard for the environment and the animals in our care.

6
Housework

Pre-War Housekeeping

Before the war, running a household was a full-time occupation for many women. Most married women did not go out to work, and routine jobs of cooking, cleaning and washing took up much of their time, for the labour-saving equipment and convenience foods that we take for granted today were not available then. In addition, standards of housework were very high, and a woman would feel it her duty to ensure that the doorstep was scrubbed white every day and

39 This photograph, taken in 1940, shows how unpleasant conditions could be in slum housing.

▼

the home thoroughly spring-cleaned each year.

In the 1930s, a woman's status in society would determine whether she did all these tasks herself, or whether she organized other people to do them for her. At one extreme, a wealthy lady would spend her time instructing the servants in their tasks and checking that these were done to her satisfaction; while at the other, a woman living in slum conditions would do hours of heavy work a day, bringing in every drop of water that she needed in a bucket from a communal outside tap, and struggling to keep the house clean with perhaps ten or more children to cope with. In homes like these, walls were often infested with bugs, and the air outside so grimy from industrial pollution that even "clean" washing came off the line dirty.

Households at both ends of society in this period make a fascinating study today.

40 Wash day in the country, carried on outdoors on a fine day! (1938).
▼

However, since there is not the space to investigate them in depth, we will look now at the general pattern of pre-war house-keeping, which the majority of women followed. Most housewives organized their work around a well-structured routine. They expected to clean, cook and shop every day, and kept special days for major tasks such as washing and baking. There were few mechanical or electrical appliances. It was common to sweep carpets with a hand brush and dustpan, for instance. Refrigerators were a rarity, so that it was difficult to keep food fresh, which is why shopping had to be done frequently. In the larder, there would be an earthenware butter cooler, and a wooden safe for meat, with a mesh door to prevent flies getting in but to allow air to circulate.

Some households did not have electricity at all, and certainly it was common to cook on a solid-fuel range and to heat rooms with coal fires. This meant a lot of work, since the ashes had to be raked out, the stove refuelled, coal carried in and fresh fires laid. Open fires and ranges produced plenty of soot and dust, which meant that it took more time to keep the rooms clean.

The family wash was usually done on a Monday, and the whole day was often set aside to cope with the washing, rinsing, "mangling", drying and ironing. The morning's activities were conducted in the scullery, a small room with a sink and a stone floor, where water could be boiled up and clothes washed in a wooden or metal tub. Soap flakes were worked up into a good lather, since there were no detergents available then. The only mechanical aids which the housewife might have for washing were paddles inside the tub, which she could turn by hand to agitate and beat the clothes, or a "dolly", a long wooden implement, looking rather like a pole with a milkmaid's stool at one end, with which she would thump and swish the washing. When the washing was finally cleaned and rinsed, it would be put through an iron mangle which

46

squeezed the water out, and then hung out to dry — always providing that the weather was fine! Most households expected cold meals only on Mondays!

A handbook of the period, which sets out to instruct the young housewife about her duties, gives an ideal timetable for daily work in the "simplest" household. How scrupulous and time-consuming it sounds today!

7 am Rise.
7.30 Lay and light the dining-room fire, if necessary.
7.45 Prepare the breakfast.
8.0 Breakfast.
8.30 Open the beds and air the rooms.
8.45 Clear away and wash up the breakfast things. Sweep and tidy the kitchen. Rub up the letter-box, sweep the porch and steps, cleaning when necessary. Polish the letter-box if of bright metal.
9.30 Lay the sitting-room fire when necessary. Sweep the dining-room and sitting-room carpets. . .mop the surrounds.
10.15 Make the beds, sweep or mop the bedroom floors. Sweep the bathroom and wc, wash the bath and lavatory basin and, if necessary, polish the taps. Sweep the landing and stairs on alternate days. Sweep and mop the hall floor.
11.0 Dust the downstairs rooms in turn, tidying up generally and replacing books, papers, renewing water in vases etc.
11.30 Prepare anything necessary for lunch and the evening meal, such as vegetables and pastry.
11.45 Shopping when necessary. Otherwise commence extra weekly duties such as ironing, turning out of rooms, metal cleaning.
12.50 Complete cooking for lunch. . . and lay the lunch.
1.15 Serve lunch.
1.45 Clear away and wash up lunch things. Clean the sink and draining boards, sweep and dust the kitchen.
2.30 Special duties or recreation, such as visiting friends, hobbies, needlework and dressmaking, golf or tennis.
4.30-5 Tea.
5.30 Prepare and cook the dinner.
7.0 Serve dinner.
8.0 Clear away and wash up, or if preferred, the washing-up could be left till morning.
(Good Housekeeping with Modern Methods, *D. D. Cottington Taylor, Good Housekeeping Magazine, 1933*).

The last suggestion seems surprisingly permissive — but perhaps even the model housewife would be too exhausted to do any more!

It is interesting to realize that before the war all middle- and upper-class households would expect to employ some help in the home. Even the working-class woman might send out her washing to be laundered, or her pies and cakes to be cooked at the baker's. The routine quoted above is that for a "servantless" household — by which the author meant a household where only one daily woman was employed, rather than any living-in help!

Housekeeping in Wartime

When the war came, many women had to do without help of any kind, and often had to go out to work themselves, to help in industry and essential war-work. They had to become very resourceful household managers, as food stuffs and commodities were in short supply. Shopping became a challenge, and often a test of endurance when long queues formed at stores where supplies had just come in.

The rumour might go round, "They're going to have liver at the butcher's — have you heard?" Everyone would rush to queue, since liver wasn't rationed. (Housewife).

The Government system of rationing ensured that what *was* available, in terms of eggs, butter, meat and dried fruit and so on, was fairly shared out. In practice, the amounts that families could obtain with their ration coupons were tiny, and housewives had to become ingenious cooks, using dried eggs instead of fresh ones, chicory and dandelion roots instead of coffee, and adapting cakes to be made without any fat and practically no sugar. The Government suggested special recipes, which often produced quite dreadful dishes! Women tried to preserve fruit and vegetables and often started keeping a few chickens in their back gardens to provide those precious eggs. Men were encouraged to "Dig for Victory" and grow as much of their own food as they could. Scrimping and saving on all household items became essential — sacks would be washed and cut up into floor cloors, and old clothes re-made into children's garments or rag mats.

Modern Convenience

The shortage of food in the war led to much research into food preservation, and this resulted in many frozen and convenience foods becoming available from the 1950s onwards. With frozen fish fingers, tinned beans, sliced bread and instant coffee, the housewife could now serve up a hot meal in a few minutes if she wanted to. Many new gadgets and pieces of equipment were marketed which took hours of drudgery out of housework. In the 1950s, for instance, twin-tub washing machines became popular, and by 1972, 73 per cent of the population owned a washing machine — often, by then, an efficient automatic model which would look after the wash from start to finish. By the 1960s nearly all homes had electricity, and families began to buy modern electric cookers, refrigerators, and later, freezers. With modern gas, electric or central heating, with fitted carpets and kitchens, cleaning became simpler and quicker.

Great progress has been made in revolutionizing the materials of which household items are made, leading to lighter and easier work for the housewife. When durable, flexible plastic was marketed in the 1950s

41   Much more scrubbing was done by hand before squeezy mops, good detergents and vinyl flooring were invented. Notice the enamel bucket. (1956).

▼

and '60s, for instance, wicker laundry
baskets, wooden plate-racks and enamel
bowls went out of use. Nylon and easy-care
fabrics were developed which needed a mini-

42   This shows an early automatic washing
machine, probably designed in the late 1950s.

▼

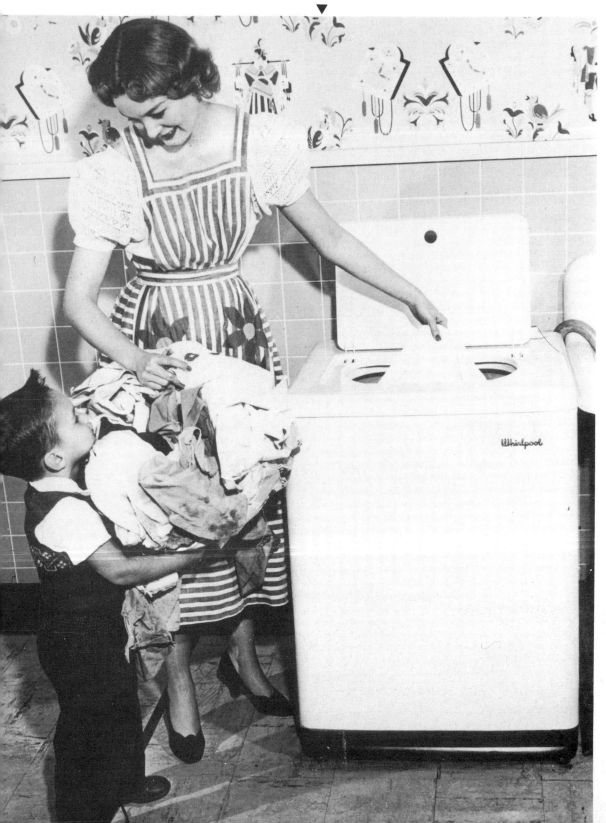

mum of washing and ironing. Even nappies, which once presented an arduous daily task of boiling and rinsing, could now be dropped into a bucket of special disinfectant and rinsed off in the machine.

For many women, housework has become of secondary importance, and their priority has become paid work outside the home. However, many too find that the dual task of keeping a job and running the home is very demanding and exhausting. Even though the trend for husbands to help in the home has grown in the last ten or fifteen years, it is usually the woman who plans and organizes the running of the home and who does the major part of the work. A growing number of women, therefore, are once again looking to paid help to make sure the house is adequately looked after.

Of course, not all women go out to work, particularly those with small children. Even those who willingly make a career out of running the home, however, find that modern equipment and fittings reduce the amount of housework needed to the point where it certainly does not fill up the whole day. Some have developed skills such as dressmaking, embroidery, upholstery or pottery, which bring back some of the creative art of home-making. Now that the novelty of convenience foods has worn off, many women find that they do in fact like to bake their own bread and cook new, interesting recipes.

In the 1980s, much of the drudgery has gone from housework. Expectations of a spotless kitchen, of beds stripped and aired daily, and of a house swept from top to bottom each morning have also gone. With modern tools and appliances, with fridge and freezer so that she can bulk-buy food, a woman can clean, cook and shop in less time than ever before. The challenge to her now is to decide what to do with the time she has

43 Advertising has had a profound influence on housewives of the post-war period. Pictures such as this (c. 1960) of a "dream kitchen" were designed to tempt women into ordering sparkling new equipment.

▼

▲
44   Food mixers have become an invaluable aid to cooking in the last 15 years.

45   Washing up as it is done today. Few homes own dishwashers and the chore is still one carried out several times a day for most housewives. Sinks are now usually made of stainless steel, and have fitted cupboards built in below.

▼

▲
46   More men help with the housework nowadays, especially when their wives go out to work as well.

left, whether to take up paid employment, to devote herself to her children, develop her own interests and talents, or work at the more creative domestic skills. There is more freedom nowadays, but the choices are not always easy.

51

7
Mining

Coal-mining is one of Britain's major industries. In 1981 around 225,000 men were employed in the process of cutting out the coal underground, bringing it to the surface, and preparing it for sale. Mining, however, is regional work, for coal seams in Britain are concentrated in the areas of northern England, lowland Scotland, and southern Wales, and these are the places where the greater proportion of mines are located. Coal itself consists of fossilized plant material formed from plants and trees which grew about 300 million years ago. There are different grades of coal, from "young" coal, which is brown and crumbly, to hard lustrous anthracite, which is compressed into a highly dense state.

Nowadays, mining is a nationalized industry, for which the National Coal Board is responsible. But until 1947, coal mines were owned privately and thus there were no national rates of pay or conditions of work. Each company employed its own workers, and in the tough economic conditions of the late 1920s and early '30s, miners often found themselves poorly paid and liable to unemployment at a moment's notice. Mining was a hazardous, dirty and badly-rewarded job. Many young men went down the pit only because they could find no other work.

From the 1930s to the 1980s, coal-mining has undergone a process of gradual mechanization which has made the work less arduous. Progress has always been quicker in some mines than in others and thus one mine may be found using an old-fashioned method of retrieving coal, while another is equipped with the latest machinery.

The 1930s

In the early 1930s, much of the coal was still hewn by hand. First of all, a "roadway" had to be made so that the men could get to the coal. This would usually involve miners working with picks, undercutting the face and propping up the passageway as they made it, with wooden pit props to prevent the ceiling collapsing. Sometimes, "firemen" would clear the first stretch with explosives. They would drill holes, pack them with the explosives, and then detonate, and the blast would bring down large quantities of rock. This was a very skilled job and a miner had to take special exams before he could become a fireman.

The tunnels made were low and narrow, and miners had to crawl along them and spend their days working in cramped conditions. Often, they wore few clothes or none, as the heat could be intense underground. Once a "road" had been established, the coal itself could be cut with hand picks and loaded into tubs. In those days ponies were kept to draw the tubs up through the passages to the place where the coal could

52

be loaded into the "cage" and transferred to the surface of the mine. Many people today think that it was cruel to keep ponies underground day and night. They only saw daylight for about two weeks of each year, when they were put out to grass for an annual holiday. But the miners were very fond of their ponies and looked after them well:

I have seen a young man, one of the toughest I ever knew, and who was capable of whipping any other man in the pit in a fight, actually in tears because his pony had been sent to another district. (Coal-Miner, G. A. W. Tomlinson, Hutchinson).

47 Hewing coal by hand, the oldest means of acquiring it.

▼

48   A miner shares his snack or "snap" with his pony.

49   Before collieries were modernized, miners washed each night at home, usually in a zinc bath, since few working-class homes had bathrooms then. (c. 1930).

At this period, miners came to work in their pit clothes and were taken down into the pit in the "cage". This is a primitive kind of lift, and the early ones were cramped and cold. A boy starting work in the pit was often given the job of "onsetter"; he would be responsible for signalling to the engine winder operator on the surface when the cage was full at the bottom of the shaft, loaded with coal or miners returning to the surface, and ready to be wound up. He had to give the signal up to 50 or 60 times an hour and could find the work "unbelievably monotonous and wearying" (Tomlinson).

After work, the men went home black and grimy to strip off and wash at home. Over the years, pithead conditions improved enormously, and in the 1940s already it was common to find showers installed, lockers provided for clothes, and canteens where a hot meals could be bought. Today, the NCB supplies working clothes for the miners and launders and repairs them free of charge.

Mining Machines

Mechanization was introduced gradually into the mines, so that by 1938 56 per cent of coal was produced with the aid of machines. First, a coal-cutter was used, which was driven by compressed air and was like a huge chain-saw; pneumatic picks were invented which enabled miners to work on seams of coal more efficiently. Conveyor belts were introduced, which could take the coal along from the face to where it could be loaded, and this meant that pit ponies were no longer in such demand. Their numbers declined dramatically through the 1940s and '50s, but it is interesting to note that a few were still in use even in the 1970s.

Over the years power-loaders have been developed. These are machines which will cut the coal and load it onto conveyors

50 Cutting coal with a pneumatic pick. The pit props are of steel.

▼

51 This is a colliery train of the 1950s, used to carry miners at the bottom of the shaft to the coal face where they were to work.

automatically, making the cutting and shifting of coal one continuous operation which can be supervised by skilled workers. Most of Britain's coal is now cut in this way, and there are many different types of these machines available, to suit different working conditions. The shearer-loader is frequently used, and this has a sensing device which helps to steer the machine along the coal seam without cutting into the floor or the roof of the tunnel. The roof supports are made of steel, and they are "self-advancing", moving to support the ceiling automatically.

The Dangers of Mining

Mining has always been a hazardous business, but much care and attention have been paid to improving safety standards over the last 50 years. Nowadays we do not accept pit casualties lightly, but in earlier days they were seen as unavoidable. This passage, written in the late 1940s, displays an attitude which would not be popular today:

> *The casualty list from our coal mine is inevitably heavy and is in every sense regrettable, but we must get it into perspective. Roughly speaking, there are as many persons killed and seriously injured on our roads in a month as there are in our collieries in a year. The latest pre-war figures showed that fatalities were approximately 850 per annum, and serious injuries about 3,000 — or, respectively, 1 and 4 persons per 1,000 employed.* (The Secrets of Other People's Jobs, Odhams Press Ltd)

The greatest danger has always been from rock falls, and safety was improved in this respect when hydraulic supports were brought in in 1945, which held up the roof much better than the old props. Safety helmets became obligatory, the earlier types, being heavy and tiring to wear, replaced in the '40s and '50s by lightweight, extra-tough ones. Ventilation, to ensure enough fresh air to breathe down in the mine, used to be controlled from furnaces, but by 1950 all these had been replaced by mechanical fans which pump air down one shaft and suck it up another. These are more efficient and reliable. The miners themselves have always been aware of the risk of their work, and an account written in 1937 includes this harrowing description of an accident:

One becomes accustomed to the sight of blood after a few years in the pits, but I shall never forget my first sight of an injured man being carried towards the pit bottom. The sweating, half-naked, cursing men carrying the broken body of their mate, stumbling over the sleepers and rails, the feeble gleam of the miner's lamps carried by other mates. . . (Tomlinson).

Mining Today

Miners have been known as a tough, proud bunch, loyal to their fellow workers and ready to stand up for their rights. In the earlier years of this century they were often badly-treated as regards pay and employment, and today they show keen fighting spirit if they consider that their conditions and wages are less than they should be. After nationalization, in 1947, facilities, rights of employment and pay improved tremendously, until by 1960 the miners were reasonably well-paid by the standard of other skilled manual workers. By the 1970s, however, their wages no longer compared so favourably, and this led to a period of industrial unrest. A series of strikes was staged, and the British public woke up to the fact that miners are still key workers, when power cuts and industrial stoppages followed as a direct result of loss of coal supplies.

At this time, too, there was uncertainty in the industry as to whether there would be a continuing need for coal. Many households had switched to gas and oil heating, and industries, too, made greater use of oil.

52 ▼ Sorting of coal was once done by hand. (1932).

The Government, in a White Paper published in 1967, made the assumption that "regular and competitively-priced supplies of oil" would continue to flow into the country. However, in the mid-1970s the price of oil rose dramatically. It was clear that coal would go on playing a major part in the nation's economy, and thus the Government actively encouraged modernization and expansion of the mines.

There is continual research today into more efficient ways of "harvesting" the coal that Britain needs. An example of modern development can be traced in the process of sorting and cleaning the coal, grading it by size and removing the surplus dust and grit so that it is ready for sale. In the 1940s, giant mechanical sieves would sort the coal into sizes, and each grade would be loaded onto a slow-moving belt. Men would sort the coal on the belt, removing stones or sub-standard pieces. Then it would be carried by wagons to the washery, where the foreman would check that the clean coal floated up to the surface while the dirt remained on the bottom. Today, fully-automated coal preparation plants have been developed where this process is electronically controlled and operators work with control panels and remote-controlled television cameras to check the progress of the coal.

More and more work in the mines can be done automatically and computers have been introduced to control coal-cutting and loading, relieving men of some of the dangerous work on the coal-face itself. A "gamma ray controlled nucleonic probe" (*Coal's New Face*, NCB publication) has been designed so that a cutter can actually sense the difference between stone and coal and will thus cut out only coal from the face. Many of these new inventions are only in limited use at the moment, but it seems plain that the trend of mine-working will be for less and less face work for miners. Men will need to be highly-skilled, but their knowledge will need to be geared to the operation of sophisticated machines.

53   This is a modern coal-cutter, which does much of the work automatically and much faster than previous methods.

▼

8
Offices

The changes which took place in office life between 1930 and the mid-'70s are minor compared to the revolution in office work that is happening today. The introduction of computers on a large scale has now begun to transform the kind of work that can be done, the skills needed by office staff, and the whole outlook of the business world.

In the pre-war period, and for many years after, offices were considered to be strictly functional places. Desks and chairs were bought for their utility rather than for comfort or beauty. The emphasis was on efficiency, with lino or wooden floors, and plain walls without posters, charts or any other "distracting" items pinned to them! It was common to have a general office, with

54　A "model" office of 1934.
▼

separate offices leading off it. The general office would be a large room, where most of the typists were installed, and the smaller offices would be for the executives or other high-level staff.

Although women had been employed in offices since Victorian times, many employers still regarded them with suspicion, or as "second-best". Certainly they would not be natural candidates for promotion into management. When Eric Pasold opened the clothing factory (later Ladybird's) in 1931 he reacted strongly to the idea of female office staff:

> *"Girls? We'll have no girls in the office!"*
> *"Not even a typist?"*
> *"No," I replied firmly, "There will only be a clerk. He will type all the letters, and the office boy will type the invoices. A girl in the office is only a distraction."*

The office boy was a legendary figure, no longer to be found after the war. He was generally thought of as a grubby, cheeky youth, who made tea, took messages, stamped the letters, and basically did all the jobs that no one else wanted to do.

There was far more typing work to do until the 1960s, when photocopiers were introduced. Until this period, too, most typewriters were manual. As for telephones, Subscriber Trunk Dialling (STD) had not been invented, which meant that all long-distance calls and even local ones in some areas had to be made through the operator.

Even fifteen years ago if we wanted to call up another branch of the firm twenty miles away, we had to book a call through the switchboard. You could wait all morning to get through. (Company executive).

Switchboards were often cumbersome and ill-sited. In Bentall's, a department store, the switchboard was kept in a small kiosk just outside the main building until the day when a runaway cow forced its way in and got stuck there, jamming all the lines and setting every telephone bell in the store ringing!

Before the war, formality in offices was strict, with bosses always addressed as "Mr" and typists and secretaries as "Miss" or "Mrs". Smart dress was expected; suits and ties were worn by men, and neat, unassuming dresses or outfits by women. Until the 1960s the idea of a secretary had very little glamour attached to it, carrying the image of a prim, tidily-dressed lady, often of mature years and with a narrow outlook on life.

Daily office hours were normally 9 till 6, and these have stayed much the same till the present day, with just an hour less being worked in most offices now. The biggest change has been in the abolition of Saturday morning work, which was expected until at least the early post-war years. Holiday periods have extended until they have grown from the week or two weeks commonly granted in the 1930s to an average of three or four weeks per year.

After the war, many new office blocks were built to replace those damaged or destroyed, and in the 1950s and '60s much attention was paid to their design. An office was still supposed to be a place where work was done efficiently, but it was now recognized that austerity and military precision in arrangement might not be the best way to achieve this.

Two main types of design were tried out, and both may still be seen in use today. One is known as the "corridor" plan, where many small offices open off a main corridor.

This has the advantage of allowing staff to work with only two or three others around them, in quieter and more private surroundings. The other is the "open-plan" office, where operations are carried out in an open room which might take up the whole of one floor of the building. The open-plan office allows desks and equipment to be moved around easily, and encourages speedy communication between personnel. However, as might be expected, it can also be noisy and distracting! The difference between the open-plan office and the old general office

56 Many young girls of the 1950s and '60s dreamed of becoming a well-dressed secretary able to take down important letters in shorthand. ▼

is that different grades of staff are likely to be working together in the open-plan. Open-plan offices can also be "landscaped", according to the amount of space each employee needs, and the "pathways" that need to be created between different areas. For instance, if Miss K needs to confer with Mrs G at least ten times a day, then it makes sense to situate them close together or to ensure that there is an easy pathway between their desks.

Even offices which were not professionally planned started to brighten up in the 1960s. Many touches of colour and comfort were added, such as plants, curtains, posters and carpets. A minimum standard was set by the Offices Shops and Railway Premises Act 1963, which ordered that a place of work should be clean, with a temperature of not less than 60.8 degrees Fahrenheit, with good ventilation, drinking water, washing facilities and lighting.

It became common for young girls in the 1950s and '60s to enter office life as typists or secretaries. Prior training and qualifications could now be obtained from schools and colleges. At this period the distinction between a typist and a secretary was very marked. A typist spent all day typing out letters, copying memoranda, and so on. A secretary was expected to have a grasp of office procedure as well as being expert at shorthand and typing. Unlike the typist, she would probably come into contact with the general public, or with visitors to the office. Although this difference still exists, it has become less pronounced:

> *Anyone can be a secretary straight away now, whereas years ago most worked their way up from copy typist. The word secretary is used too loosely today. (Manager's Secretary).*

Temporary workers have become a feature of office life. Several factors led to this. In the 1960s many city offices found themselves short of staff, with jobs being plentiful and the cost of travel to the city centre escalating. Longer holidays, too, meant that staff were frequently absent. Thus temporary help was needed to fill in where necessary. Many men and women liked the idea of moving from job to job, and temporary rates of pay were good. "Temps" can take their holidays when they choose — although they will not be paid for these — and temporary work is especially suitable for mothers who want to work only during school terms.

Other alterations in the structure of work have been the introduction of "flexitime" and "job sharing". These have been adopted cautiously by certain firms over the last ten years or so, and it is hard to say at the

57   In the early 1970s pocket calculators became widely available and office workers dealing with figures have found them invaluable ever since.

▼

moment whether they will become more popular or peter out. "Flexitime" is a system whereby office staff can choose, to some extent, when they fit their 8 hours of work into the day. A person might, for instance, prefer to start work at 7 am, so beating the morning traffic jams, and leave for home at 3 pm. Job sharing, a newer venture, is a way of allowing two people to fill one post. Two married women might agree to work 2½ days each, thus making up a full working week between them.

Office standards have become much more informal over the last twenty years. However, whereas an advertising office will have staff who dress as they please, in jeans or fashionable clothes, and address each other by their Christian names, a solicitor's office is likely to expect staff to arrive soberly dressed — women *not* in trousers — and to keep a respectful attitude to each other and to their superiors.

▲
58   This is a modern typing pool. The arrangement is formal, but there are plants on the window sill, the floor is carpeted and the chairs look as though they give good support to the typists' backs. Some of the women are using audio equipment so that they can type straight from a recorded tape.

It is the computer that is creating major changes in office life. Although computers have been available for over twenty years, they were too expensive, bulky and limited in their application until the mid '70s. Since then, phenomenal developments have been made in their construction, allowing the inexpensive "desk-top" computer to come into common use, with its TV screen display and its keyboard (like that of a typewriter) to programme and extract information. Basically, this means that many time-consuming jobs of book-keeping, administration, research and duplicating can now be done by the computer in a fraction of the time they

64

59   Electronics have revolutionized the switchboards of offices. Now there are no more tangled wires and plugs and the equipment is more reliable and efficient.

previously took. A computer for a large store can automatically calculate the amount of stock sold, and of what type. An insurance company can feed the name of a client into its computer and obtain instant full information as to his investments. Perhaps the most crucial feature, in relation to typists, is that the computer can now print out letters by the thousand. The insurance company wishing, for instance, to advise its investors of a new savings scheme or to reply to new enquiries, can programme its computer to issue a standard letter with the individual's name included, rather than instructing the typist to spend a whole day writing personally to all those on the mailing list whose names begin with "B"! The director of one such company predicted: "In two years time, there will be hardly any conventional typewriters in this office." He also stressed the growing dependence upon the computer, however, with the need for speedy repairs should anything go wrong, for "the office can't afford to have it out of action for even a single day." Computers

generate other problems, too. To avoid the risk of loss through fire, duplicate tapes and discs must be kept in a fire-proof safe. Means have to be devised of keeping information secure from rival firms or from staff who have no right of access to it. This problem is usually overcome by introducing a personal code system, whereby the computer will only operate if you tap your personal password into it first.

For some firms, this is going to mean the loss of jobs among clerical and secretarial staff. On the other hand, some find that the efficiency of computers generates extra business, and thus they still need all of their staff. Many will be re-trained to use computer terminals. Indeed, large numbers of staff find that the use of computers has improved the quality of their jobs. The reduction of repetitive, monotonous work and the introduction of instant information-retrieval facilities mean that they can tackle new problems and challenges which would previously have been beyond their scope.

60   The most important piece of equipment today is the computer. Most are about the size of the one pictured here.
▼

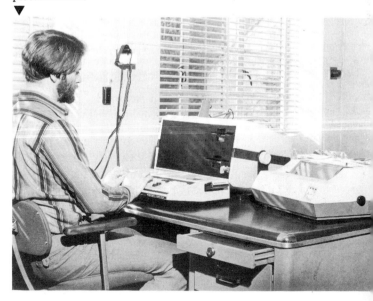

Date List

1930   Road Traffic Act. This laid down regulations about how many hours a bus or lorry
        driver could work at a stretch. It also controlled the way bus companies were
        organized, ensuring that they had proper routes and timetables.
1931   Jarrow Hunger March.
        Introduction of Means Test.
1939-1945   Second World War. Recruitment of men into the armed forces and shortages of
        goods radically affected most people's employment.
1941   Younger women without children called up by Government to do war work.
1945-1951   Labour Government in power. They introduced nationalization schemes for
        transport and industry.
1946   National Insurance Act. This required the working population to pay fixed contri-
        butions towards pensions, sickness and unemployment benefits.
1947   Coal mines and railways nationalized.
1955   Railway Modernization Plan. This initiated the changeover from steam to diesel.
1956   Clean Air Act. The release of smoke into the atmosphere from factories and private
        homes could now be controlled, which gradually led to cleaner and healthier working
        and living conditions.
1963   Contracts of Employment Act. This laid down minimum periods of notice to be
        given by employer or worker.
        Beeching Report. Dr Beeching's plan to shut down small and unprofitable railway
        lines was implemented, severely affecting jobs and transport in rural areas.
        Offices Shops and Railway Premises Act. It lays down the conditions under which
        most businesses must be run, making adequate heating, ventilation, and cleaning
        compulsory.
        Location of Offices Bureau established; a Government-backed project which aimed
        to encourage firms to move their offices out of Central London to rural and provincial
        locations.
        Invention of the silicon chip, which later (1970s) became the essential factor in the
        computer revolution.
1965   Redundancy Payments Act. Workers made redundant now had the right to extra pay-
        ments from their employers, the amount depending upon salary and length of
        employment.
1968   Race Relations Act. This made it illegal for employers to discriminate against a person

on grounds of race or colour.

1970 Equal Pay Act. This law was introduced to try to ensure that women were paid on the same basis as men. "Like pay for like work" is the theme of the law; previously, employers could offer women lower wages than men for the same job.

1971 Decimalization of British currency. Many firms arranged special training schemes for their staff, to teach them how to use the new system.

1973 Britain entered the Common Market. This has altered the grants and subsidy schemes which affect agriculture in this country.
      Value Added Tax (VAT) introduced, a tax on goods and services which must be collected by the person supplying them. This has meant a great deal more work for the small businessman and shopkeeper.

1974 Health and Safety at Work Act. This requires employers to take adequate measures to protect their employees from injury and disease.

1975 Employment Protection Act. This makes several important provisions, including maternity leave and pay for women employees, the right to time off with pay to perform union duties, and guaranteed minimum payments for workers who are temporarily laid-off or put on short-time.
      Sex Discrimination Act. This Act makes it illegal to refuse employment simply on grounds of sex; although it is usually women who are discriminated against, there have been cases of men being refused work too! It also obliges the employer to give equal opportunities in terms of promotion and training to men and women. However, there are many occupations and situations which are excluded from the law, cases in which it is thought reasonable that a woman is more suitable than a man, or vice versa.

Glossary

Computer General term for machines developed over the last 25 years which can perform exceedingly complex calculations. Computers have "memory" which stores information and sequences needed for different "programmes" of operation.

Conveyor belt A moving belt usually found in factories, which carries along the articles being made through each stage of the manufacturing process.

Inflation The term given to a phase in economy when money loses some of its value. In other words, in an inflationary period, goods which cost £1 a year ago may cost £1.20 today.

Means Test The old Government system of deciding whether people should be given money when they were sick or out of work. It was used in the 1930s and its intention was to assess if the person in question had any goods or resources which could raise money; if so, then the Government would not pay out. It was applied very harshly.

Mechanization The process of inventing machines to do tasks which were previously done by hand or with simple tools.

National Insurance The modern scheme of state benefits. Contributions are compulsorily paid by those who work and their employers, and funds will be paid out in times of sickness, unemployment and so on.

Nationalization An industry is said to be nationalized when it is owned by the state; any profits made belong to the nation and not to individuals. Gas, electricity and the Post Office are examples of nationalized industries.

Pension Usually refers to an "old-age pension", which is a regular payment of money made to those above retiring age. There are both state and private pension schemes and the money to be paid out later is collected during all or some of the years of working life.

Piece rates Payment for work completed rather than for time spent at work.

Private enterprise A business of any kind which is run by individuals or by a company which is not state-owned.

Quality Circles New schemes designed to encourage workers to use their talents to create ideas and solve problems within the firm.

Rationing A system introduced by the Government during the war to share out goods fairly, since many were in short supply.

Recession A period when it is hard for businesses to make money, and thus unemployment is likely to be a problem.

Trades Unions Independent organizations made up of working people who elect representatives to discuss problems with management and negotiate pay rises and better working conditions. Almost half Britain's employees belong to a union.

Places to Visit

There are many opportunities to visit places of work and see how they are run today, and perhaps to speak to some of the older employees and ask them about changes they have experienced. With shops and factories, it is best to contact the Personnel Manager or Publicity Officer in advance and ask if a tour can be made. In some areas there are working farms which are open to the public at certain times. Museums of Industry and Museums of Rural Life can be interesting to visit, giving plenty of information about working life in the past.

Few coal mines accept visitors today, but the Chatterley Whitfield Mining Museum, near Stoke-on-Trent provides marvellous tours of a real mine no longer in use. Many of the guides have worked as miners and can describe life down the pit in years gone by.

An excellent reference book is *See Britain at Work* by A. Langsbury (Exley Publications, 1977-81). This gives details of all kinds of farms, factories, businesses, museums and so on which the public can visit, with information about times of opening, charges, any need to book in advance and so on.

Books for Further Reading

Rowan Bentall,
My Store of Memories
W. H. Allen, 1974
(The story of Bentall's Department Store)

Alan Delgado,
The Enormous File,
John Murray, 1979
(A history of office life)

Man of the Southern: Jim Evans Looks Back,
Allen and Unwin, 1980
(Memories of life working on the railways)

James Herriot,
All Creatures Great and Small,
Pan
(Reminiscences of a vet, giving insight into
life on Yorkshire farms in the 1930s. Also
see other books by James Herriot)

Kenneth Hudson and John Baker,
Where We Used To Work,
1980

Kenneth Hudson and Julian Pettifer,
Diamonds in the Sky,
Bodley Head/BBC, 1979
(A social history of flying)

Frank Huggett,
Factory Life and Work,
Harrap, 1973

For Older Readers

British Agriculture Today,
An Association of Agriculture Production,
1978

Clive Jenkins and Barry Sherman,
The Collapse of Work,
Methuen, 1979
(A survey of the implications of modern
technology on the pattern of work today)

Trades Unions
Central Office of Information,
Ref. pamphlet 12, 1975

Index

71